Modern World Religions
Sikhism

Jon Mayled

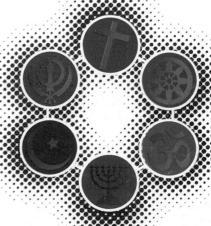

Heinemann Educational Publishers
Halley Court, Jordan Hill, Oxford, OX2 8EJ
Part of Harcourt Education

Heinemann is the registered trademark of
Harcourt Education Limited

First published in 2002

06 05 04
10 9 8 7 6 5 4 3 2

British Library Cataloguing in Publication Data
A catalogue record for this book is available from the
British Library

ISBN 0 435 33627 4

Picture research by Jennifer Johnson
Typeset by Artistix, Thame, Oxon
Illustrated by Artistix
Printed and bound in Spain by Edelvives

Acknowledgements
The publishers would like to thank the following for
permission to use photographs:

The Environmental Picture Library/Graham Burns, p. 50;
TRIP/H. Luther, pp. 45, 56; TRIP/Resource Foto, p. 48;
TRIP/H. Rogers, pp. 2, 5, 6, 7, 8, 9, 10 (right), 12, 13, 19,
20 (both), 21, 23, 24, 25, 28, 29, 49, 52, 54, 55, 58, 59;
Harjinder Singh Sagoo, pp. 3, 10 (left), 14, 15, 18, 26, 27,
30, 31, 32, 33, 34, 35, 36, 37, 38, 40, 41, 42, 43, 44, 46, 47,
53, 57; TRIP/R. Westlake, p. 51.

The publishers have made every effort to contact
copyright holders. However, if any material has been
incorrectly acknowledged, the publishers would be
pleased to correct this at the earliest opportunity.

Websites
Links to appropriate websites are given throughout the
pack. Although these were up-to-date at the time of
writing, it is essential for teachers to preview these sites
before using them with pupils. This will ensure that the
web address (URL) is still accurate and the content is
suitable for your needs. We suggest that you bookmark
useful sites and consider enabling pupils to access them
through the school intranet. We are bringing this to your
attention as we are aware of legitimate sites being
appropriated illegally by people wanting to distribute
unsuitable and offensive material. We strongly advise
you to purchase suitable screening software so that
pupils are protected from unsuitable sites and their
material. If you do find that the links given no longer
work, or the content is unsuitable, please let us know.
Details of changes will be posted on our website.

Tel: 01865 888058   www.heinemann.co.uk

Contents

An introduction to Sikhism

In this section you will:

● learn about and understand what faith and trust mean

● consider the ways in which Sikhism seeks to strengthen faith in Waheguru (God)

● think about and share your opinions on some of the aims of Sikhism.

Faith and trust

The people who follow Sikhism are called **Sikhs**. The word 'Sikh' means a disciple, someone who tries to follow the teachings of a particular leader. In the case of Sikhism, these are the teachings of the **Gurus**.

All Sikhs have faith and trust in God, called **Waheguru** – Wonderful Lord, the God who created all things.

Like all other religions, Sikhism is based on a system of beliefs. Beliefs are things that people think to be true, even if there is little evidence to support the beliefs.

Believing in something means that a person has faith and trust in what they believe. Faith is a firm and honest belief that goes beyond all else. Trust is the certainty that what a person believes is right, a complete confidence in something, or a certainty that we will not be let down. For example, we may trust our friends.

*Poster showing the ten Gurus and the **Guru Granth Sahib Ji***

A way of life

Sikhs believe that their religion is a way of life. They believe that God created all things, and that God provided guidance to help all people live good lives according to the beliefs of Sikhism. So, to be a true Sikh means to accept God and to carry out God's will.

Sikhism teaches that all people are equal in the eyes of God and each other. One of the main aims of Sikhism is that there should be a united human society living together in peace and equality and following the teachings of God. In particular, Sikhs believe in **sewa** – selfless service for others.

Sikhism intends to give freedom of thought to all believers. It aims to free people from the round of rebirth by helping them to reach **mukti**, or spiritual freedom in their lives. They do this by responding to God with love and obedience.

Like other religions, Sikhism also aims to free the human self from vanity and greed, from envy and tension, from fear and insecurity. Through following the teachings of God, Sikhism seeks to free people from the worship of false gods and low desires, and shows them the beautiful hope of goodness and excellence leading to spiritual liberation, or freedom. Sikhism fills the heart with love for God and for all God's creation.

Sikhs are certain of their faith because they believe that God has told people about Waheguru through the teachings of the Gurus.

The first of these Gurus was **Guru Nanak Dev Ji**. To show respect to the Gurus, Sikhs add the words Ji or Dev Ji, meaning 'Honoured Sir' to the names of the Gurus. The word 'Guru' has two syllables – the first, 'gu', means darkness and the second, 'ru', means light. A Guru is, therefore, someone who helps others pass from darkness to light.

Sikh women in the gurdwara

Learning about religion

❶ **a** In pairs, discuss what the words 'faith' and 'trust' mean in Sikhism.

   b Write down your ideas, then discuss them with the class.

   c Write down the final definitions you decide on.

❷ **a** How do Sikhs use faith, trust and friendship to strengthen their belief In God?

   b Why might it be right to say that Sikhism is based on the principles of faith and friendship?

❸ **a** Write down the main aims of Sikhism.

   b Add other aims to your list as you work through this book.

Learning from religion

❶ **a** Make a list of people who you could say you have trusted or have faith in.

   b Explain why you have chosen these particular people.

❷ What effect does faith have on people's lives?

❸ Do you think that people trust each other enough? Explain your answer.

Guru Nanak Dev Ji 1

In this section you will:

● begin to learn about the Sikh Gurus

● find out about the early life of Guru Nanak Dev Ji

● start to understand the teachings that he gave to his followers.

There are six major religions in the world: Buddhism, Christianity, Hinduism, Islam, Judaism and Sikhism. Sikhism, the youngest of these religions, was founded by **Guru Nanak Dev Ji** in the fifteenth century.

The **Sikh** faith was revealed through the teachings of the ten **Gurus**. They are all respected by Sikhs, but they are not worshipped because they were human beings, not gods. As well as the Gurus, Sikhs also recognize that there have been other messengers from God such as the Buddha, Jesus and Muhammad (pbuh).

Sikhs believe that the Gurus were all very special people who did not need to be reborn, but were sent back to earth to become God's messengers.

All the Gurus taught that there is only one God, that all people are equally important before God and that everyone can attain **mukti** (spiritual liberation) through living their lives with love, and being faithful and obedient to God.

Guru Nanak Dev Ji's childhood

Guru Nanak Dev Ji was born in 1469 at Talwandi in the Punjab. Talwandi was later renamed Nankana Sahib in his honour and is now in Pakistan.

When he was born, the astrologers said that he would grow up to be someone very special who would lead other people towards God.

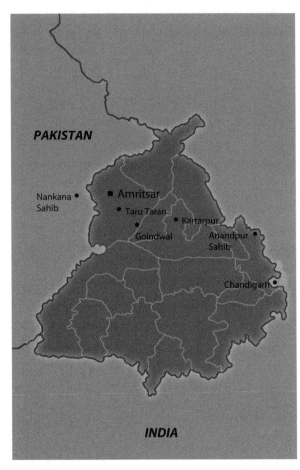

Map of north-west India showing the modern-day Punjab

Nanak's father, Mehta Kalu, was a Hindu and so he brought up his son to follow this religion. However, from an early age Nanak rejected the many rituals and customs that are part of Hinduism and other religions.

When he was five years old, he was sent to school. His teacher, Gopal Das, wrote the letters of the alphabet on a slate and Nanak asked what each letter meant. The teacher said that the letters themselves did not mean anything and he asked Nanak what he thought the letters meant. Nanak went through the alphabet and used each letter as the start of a verse of poetry in praise of God. This hymn can be read today in the Sikh scriptures, the **Guru Granth Sahib Ji**. The teacher was amazed at his pupil's understanding of God and his command of language. He realized at once that Nanak was no ordinary child, but a messenger of God.

When a Hindu boy reaches the age of about eleven he is given a sacred thread to wear. Nanak refused to wear it, saying that a thread could break, and that what he wanted was 'that sacred thread which after the death of a man accompanies his soul to the next world'.

Nanak said: 'Make kindness the material, and spin the thread of contentment. Tie knots of truth and virtue. These qualities in a person are the real sacred thread.'

On one occasion, Nanak's father sent him to a nearby town and gave him some money, which he was told to spend wisely. On the way he met some holy men. He asked them how they could live without food, homes or jobs. The men told him that they had no need of these things because God provided for them. Nanak thought about this and, when he arrived at the town, he spent his money on food for the men.

When Nanak returned home, his father was angry because he had intended that his son should invest the money, not give it away.

Guru Nanak Dev Ji, the first Guru

Learning about religion

❶ a Discuss with a friend what you understand by the words 'respect' and 'worship'.

   b Write down your ideas, then discuss them with the class.

   c Write down the final definitions you decide on.

❷ a Describe one important event from Guru Nanak Dev Ji's early life.

   b What made people think that Nanak was a very special person?

❸ a Write down what Nanak said about the sacred thread.

   b Explain why this teaching was so important.

Learning from religion

❶ a What do you think are the right ways to use money?

   b Explain why you have chosen these particular ways.

❷ Explain why it might be important for people to give money to others.

❸ Do you think the world would be different if more people followed Nanak's example?

Guru Nanak Dev Ji 2

In this section you will:

- develop an understanding of the importance of Guru Nanak Dev Ji's life and work
- consider the ways in which Sikhism stresses equality
- express your own opinions on some of the aims of Sikhism.

One of the most important events in the life of **Guru Nanak Dev Ji** happened when he was 30 years old. Early every morning, Nanak went to the river to bathe and to pray. One day he did not return at his usual time. His friends went to the river and found his clothes on the bank, but there was no sign of Nanak. Three days later, he reappeared at the same place, but said nothing of what had happened to him during this period.

After this event, Guru Nanak Dev Ji left his home and family, and travelled around the country teaching and preaching. He said that the way in which he lived was the way that God wanted. He travelled for twenty years, and visited Hindu and Muslim holy places on his journeys.

Guru Nanak Dev Ji taught that everyone should worship the same God, and that every person was equal and should be treated equally. He said there was 'no Hindu and no Muslim because everyone was equal in God's eyes'.

Guru Nanak Dev Ji said that those who followed him should always be prepared to work hard in order to serve God. He taught that human life is our chance to meet the creator, God, through having absolute love and devotion to God.

Guru Nanak Dev Ji also taught that arrogance, pride, lust, anger, greed and concerns about possessions all take us away from God.

He showed people that rituals, idol worship, prejudice about people's **caste** (the belief that people are born into different groups), and any type of oppression was wrong and would prevent people reaching God.

Guru Nanak Dev Ji visited many Hindu holy places on his travels, including Varanasi in India

could continue his work. He found Lehna to be the 'purest of the pure', and chose him even above his own two sons.

He called together **Sikhs** from across the country and blessed Lehna, giving him the name Angad, which means 'part of me'. He then announced that, from that day, Bhai Lehna would be known as Guru Angad Dev Ji, the second Guru.

Guru Angad Dev Ji, the second Guru

In 1520 Guru Nanak Dev Ji went to live in the village of Kartarpur in the Punjab and here he set up the first Sikh community.

A man called Bhai Lehna was making a pilgrimage to a Hindu shrine when he met Guru Nanak Dev Ji. He was very impressed by Guru Nanak Dev Ji's teachings and became one of his closest followers.

Lehna decided to visit Guru Nanak Dev Ji at Kartarpur. He was wearing his best clothes as he approached the village. The people were gathering grass in the fields and there was one very muddy bundle left. Lehna picked up the bundle and carried it to the village. Guru Nanak Dev Ji's wife was horrified to see the visitor carrying the muddy bundle, but Guru Nanak Dev Ji told her that it was not a bundle of grass but 'a crown to honour the best of men'.

After this, Lehna never left Guru Nanak Dev Ji, choosing to serve him in every way he could.

When Guru Nanak Dev Ji realized that he was about to die, he decided to test the faith of each of his followers in order to choose someone who

Learning about religion

❶ In your notes, suggest what might have happened when Guru Nanak Dev Ji disappeared. What happened after this event?

❷ **a** Describe what happened when Bhai Lehna visited Kartapur.

  b What was so significant about Lehna picking up the muddy bundle of grass?

❸ **a** Write down what Guru Nanak Dev Ji said about Bhai Lehna.

  b Explain why Guru Nanak Dev Ji chose Lehna to be his successor.

Learning from religion

❶ **a** What do you think is the importance of Guru Nanak Dev Ji's statement that there was 'no Hindu and no Muslim'?

  b How do you think people today might put this statement into practice?

❷ Explain why it might be important today for people to avoid arrogance, pride, lust, anger, greed and concerns about possessions.

❸ Explain what lessons you think people today could learn from Guru Nanak Dev Ji's teachings.

The Gurus 1

In this section you will:

● learn about the lives of some of the other Sikh Gurus

● learn about the teachings of these Gurus

● consider how their example might influence people's lives.

Guru Angad Dev Ji (1539–52)

Guru Angad Dev Ji collected together all the hymns of **Guru Nanak Dev Ji** and wrote them down, along with some of his own, in the **Gurmukhi** script. Gurmukhi is the name given to the script in which the scriptures and the Punjabi language are written.

Guru Angad Dev Ji encouraged **Sikhs** to take part in sport regularly, believing that a healthy body and a healthy mind were both important to God.

Guru Amar Das Ji (1552–74)

Bhai Amar Das was 60 years old when he met Guru Angad Dev Ji. He was a devout Hindu, but the truth of the teachings in the Guru's **shabads** (hymns) made him realize that God could only be served through true devotion and love, and so he changed his whole way of life. He served Guru Angad Dev Ji for thirteen years.

Every day he collected water from the River Beas for the Guru's bath. He loved the Guru so much that he would not even turn his back on him, so he walked backwards for the six-mile journey through forests to the river.

Guru Amar Das Ji became Guru when he was 73 years old. He encouraged the use of the **langar**, or Guru's kitchen, to carry on Guru Nanak Dev Ji's tradition of communal eating. He also asked his followers to come to his headquarters in **Goindwal** three times a year on the dates of important Hindu festivals.

Guru Ram Das Ji (1574–81)

Guru Ram Das Ji founded the sacred city of **Amritsar**. He was the son-in-law of Guru Amar Das Ji, and took over from him in 1574 at the age of 40. Guru Ram Das Ji invited people from 52 different trades to come to Amritsar and start new businesses in the 'Guru's Market'. He also composed the **Lavan**, which is a special hymn sung at Sikh weddings and a central part of the marriage service. He died at the age of 57.

Guru Arjan Dev Ji (1581–1606)

Guru Arjan Dev Ji was the fifth Guru, and the youngest son of Guru Ram Das Ji. Guru Arjan Dev Ji built the **Harimandir Sahib** at Amritsar, now called the Golden Temple, in the middle of the lake constructed by the fourth Guru. He also built **gurdwaras** at the great cities of Taru Taran, Kartarpur and Shri Hargobindpur.

The Golden Temple at Amritsar

Guru Arjan Dev Ji

Guru Arjan Dev Ji collected together the hymns of the first four Gurus, along with some of his own, in a volume called the **Adi Granth**. Sikhs believe that the Gurus' hymns are the words of God and, therefore, these holy scriptures are treated with utmost respect. Once the Adi Granth was completed and placed in the Harimandir, Guru Arjan Dev Ji slept on the floor of the temple, to show his love and respect for the word of God.

Guru Arjan Dev Ji was the first Sikh martyr. The Mogul emperor Jehangir was jealous of the Guru's fame and following. Even some devout Muslims were praising the Guru's saintliness. At his court, Jehangir tried to convert Guru Arjan Dev Ji to Islam under the threat of death.

Guru Arjan Dev Ji refused, and was tortured and martyred. The torture lasted for five days. The Guru was first placed in a tank of boiling water. The next day, he had to sit on a plate of red-hot iron. On the third day, red-hot sand was poured over his blistered body. Guru Arjan Dev Ji remained calm and peaceful throughout his

ordeal to show that all people should happily accept the will of God. Before his death, Guru Arjan Dev Ji sent a message that his son Har Gobind was to become the sixth Guru. He said that as peaceful means had failed with the Emperor, it was now right to use the sword to protect the weak and innocent, so he instructed Guru Har Gobind Ji to carry weapons.

Learning about religion

❶ a In your notes, explain the main events in the life of Guru Arjan Dev Ji.

  b Why were the events of his life so important?

❷ a Describe how Guru Amar Das Ji served Guru Angad Dev Ji.

  b What does the fact that he walked backwards and collected water for him tell you about the respect Guru Amar Dev Ji had for Guru Angad Dev Ji ?

❸ Why do you think that Guru Amar Das Ji encouraged his followers to visit him three times a year?

Learning from religion

❶ a What is your opinion about the teaching that God wants his followers to have a healthy body as well as a healthy mind?

  b Do you think that people should put this idea into practice today?

❷ Explain why it might be important to serve other people in the way that Guru Amar Das Ji served Guru Angad Dev Ji.

❸ Explain what lessons could be learnt from the example of Guru Arjan Dev Ji.

The Gurus 2

In this section you will:

- learn about the lives of some more of the Sikh Gurus
- learn about the teachings of these Gurus
- consider how their example might influence people's lives.

Guru Har Gobind Ji (1606–44)

Guru Har Gobind Ji was the only son of Guru Arjan Dev Ji. He was eleven years old when his father was executed and he became the sixth Guru.

Guru Har Gobind Ji is sometimes called the 'Warrior Guru' because, after his father's death, instead of wearing the traditional prayer beads, he wore two **kirpans**, or swords. One sword represented spiritual power, and the other worldly power. These two swords appeared on the flags of his army and are now on the Sikh flag, the **Nishan Sahib**.

Guru Har Gobind Ji trained **Sikhs** to fight in order to defend themselves if necessary. He had a small army and fought against the Mogul emperor on several occasions.

Even today some Sikhs in India still wear 'warrior uniform'.

Guru Har Rai Ji (1644–61)

Guru Har Rai Ji was fourteen years old when he became the seventh Guru. His father instructed him that he should always have 2200 soldiers and horses with him.

Guru Har Rai Ji is also remembered for setting up a system so that free medicines were given to those who were sick. Today, some of the large **gurdwaras** in India continue to give free medical treatment to the poor.

Guru Har Rai Ji

Sikhs holding the Nishan Sahib

The Emperor of India asked Guru Har Rai Ji to come and explain his hymns. He sent his son, Ram Rai, instead, instructing him that not one word of the hymns could be changed because they are the words of God. However, Ram Rai was tested by the Emperor and finally broke the rules his father had given him. Because of this, Guru Har Rai Ji declared that the next Guru would be his youngest son, Har Krishan.

Guru Har Krishan Ji (1661–4)

Guru Har Krishan Ji was only five years old when he succeeded his father and he is sometimes called the 'Child Guru'. He died of smallpox at the age of eight and named his great uncle as his successor. While he was dying, many people who also had smallpox were healed when they drank spring water that he gave to them.

There is a famous gurdwara called Bangla Sahib at the site of Guru Har Krishan Ji's place of death in Delhi.

Guru Tegh Bahadur Ji (1664–75)

Guru Tegh Bahadur Ji was given his name, which means 'brave sword', to replace his birth name Tyag Mal. He was the youngest son of Guru Har Gobind Ji.

Many people plotted against Guru Tegh Bahadur Ji. He fought against the Mogul rulers who were destroying Sikh temples and forcing people to convert to Islam. The Emperor had made Sikhs and Hindus pay large taxes, and had closed their schools and temples. Guru Tegh Bahadur Ji fought against the Emperor and was arrested.

Four of the Guru's companions were executed while he was made to watch because they would not convert to Islam. Then he was also killed.

Guru Tegh Bahadur Ji is respected because he died protecting the liberty of both Sikhs and Hindus. He was 54 years old when he died, and a gurdwara called Sis Ganj Sahib now stands in the square in Delhi where he was executed.

Learning about religion

❶ a Describe the origins of the Sikh flag, the Nishan Sahib.

   b Explain one of the reasons why Guru Har Rai Ji is remembered today.

❷ a Why did Guru Har Rai Ji not choose his eldest son to succeed him as Guru?

   b Explain the importance of one event in the life of Guru Har Krishan Ji.

❸ Why is Guru Tegh Bahadur Ji regarded with such respect?

Learning from religion

❶ a What can we learn about obedience from the story of Ram Rai?

   b In what ways should people be obedient today?

❷ Explain why it might be important to stand up for freedom as Guru Tegh Bahadur Ji did.

❸ What can we learn from the example of Guru Tegh Bahadur Ji about the way in which we treat people of other religions?

Guru Gobind Singh Ji

Guru Gobind Singh Ji (1666–1708)

Guru Gobind Singh Ji was nine years old when his father Guru Tegh Bahadur Ji was executed and he had to take on the role of Guru. He was the last human Guru, and probably the most famous after **Guru Nanak Dev Ji**.

Guru Gobind Rai Ji, as he was originally known, was a very clever linguist and a skilled horseman, archer and hunter. He was also a great poet, and a book of his poems called the **Dasam Granth** (the Tenth Collection) is second in importance to the **Guru Granth Sahib Ji** itself.

Guru Gobind Rai Ji is remembered for two very important contributions to Sikhism.

He formed the **Khalsa**, the 'community of the pure', and he chose the **Adi Granth**, now called the Guru Granth Sahib Ji, to succeed him and to be the final Guru.

The Khalsa

In 1699 **Sikhs** from all over the Punjab were gathered at Anandpur, which is in a valley at the foot of the Himalayas, to follow the instructions of Guru Amar Das Ji. This was **Baisakhi**, the time of the Hindu festival of the wheat harvest, which is celebrated on 13 April (or on 14 April, once every 36 years).

Guru Gobind Rai Ji gave a new meaning to Baisakhi for Sikhs.

He asked for five volunteers who would give up their life for their faith. Each man went into a tent and the Guru then came out with blood on his sword. After the fifth man had gone inside, the tent was opened to show that all five were alive and well.

These men, the **panj piare**, or 'Five Beloved Ones', had been prepared to die for their faith. This event marked the founding of the Khalsa – the community of the pure. From now on, all Sikhs were encouraged to wear the **panj kakke** – five Ks. Guru Gobind Rai Ji also said that all Sikh males should take the name **Singh**, meaning 'lion', and that Sikh females should take the name **Kaur**, which means 'princess'. He then changed his name to Guru Gobind Singh Ji. He dissolved sugar crystals in water and stirred it with a **khanda** (a double-edged sword). Then he sprinkled it over the panj piare.

Guru Gobind Singh Ji with his sons

The Guru Granth Sahib Ji is the final Sikh Guru

The events at Baisakhi in 1699 marked the founding of the Khalsa and since then, the festival of Baisakhi has been the beginning of the Sikh New Year.

Guru Gobind Singh Ji and his followers in Anandpur were constantly under attack from the Mogul armies, and he and his wife were forced to leave. Many battles were fought between the Khalsa and the Moguls. During these battles, Guru Gobind Singh Ji lost his four sons and his mother. Countless numbers of Sikhs were killed, but this did not stop more and more Sikhs from joining the ranks of the Khalsa.

Guru Gobind Singh Ji died of stab wounds in 1708.

The Guru Granth Sahib Ji

When he was lying on his death bed, Guru Gobind Singh Ji took five coins and a coconut. He placed these in front of the Adi Granth. This was the way in which a new Guru was given office, and so, by doing this, he was naming the Adi Granth as his successor. From then on, the Adi Granth was known as the Guru Granth Sahib Ji.

Learning about religion

1　**a**　What skills did Guru Gobind Rai Dev Ji have?

　　b　Explain one of the reasons that Guru Gobind Singh Ji is remembered today.

2　Explain the importance of the panj piare.

3　**a**　How was a new Guru given office?

　　b　Why do you think that Guru Gobind Singh Ji chose the Guru Granth Sahib Ji to succeed him?

Learning from religion

1　**a**　What can we learn about faith from the story of the panj piare?

　　b　In what ways might people show faith today?

2　Explain why it might be important to stand up for your faith or beliefs.

3　What can we learn from the example of Guru Gobind Singh Ji?

Sikh leaders

There are no priests in Sikhism as in some other religions, but there is a person who is responsible for leading the services.

Anyone who is a member of the **Khalsa** can read from the **Guru Granth Sahib Ji**, but it is usual for a **gurdwara** to have a person who is specially trained to read from Guru Granth Sahib Ji. This person is called a **granthi**, or 'reader', and can be either a man or a woman.

The granthi is also responsible for looking after the Guru Granth Sahib Ji.

In some gurdwaras, the granthi is employed full time and this is funded by the local community. In larger gurdwaras in India, and in many of those in the UK, the granthi works for the gurdwara full time. In small villages in the Punjab and elsewhere, most granthis are part time and have other jobs.

As well as reading from the Guru Granth Sahib Ji, the granthi is also responsible for organizing the ceremonies in the gurdwara.

However, even when there is a full-time granthi, other people may read from the Guru Granth Sahib Ji and may also lead the worship and the singing.

In addition to being responsible for worship in the gurdwara, some granthis may visit the sick and needy and comfort those who are mourning a death. However, even when there is a granthi, these duties also belong to the whole of the **Sikh** community.

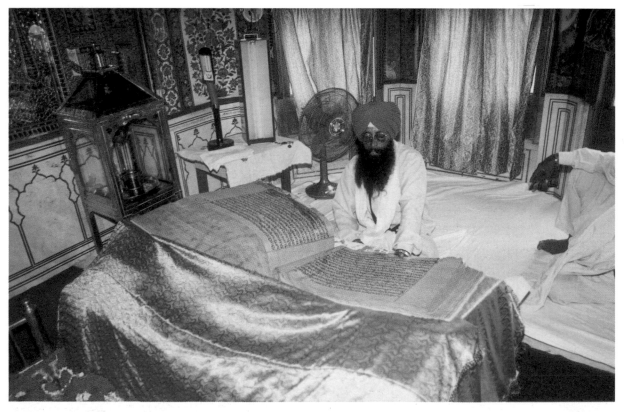

A granthi reading from the Guru Granth Sahib Ji

Ragis perform an important role in the gurdwara

Along with the granthi, the **ragi** is also an important person in the gurdwara. During services, a ragi sits to the side of the Guru Granth Sahib Ji and provides music for singing. The most common instruments are the baja, which is like a harmonium, and a tabla or jorri, which is a drum.

Learning about religion

❶ **a** What is a granthi?

b Explain the contribution a granthi makes to a Sikh community.

❷ **a** What are the different duties of a granthi?

b Why might some of these duties be shared among the rest of the Sikh community?

❸ Why do you think ragis are important in a gurdwara?

Learning from religion

❶ Why might it be helpful if everyone could read from holy books?

❷ Explain why it might be helpful if religious duties were shared within a community.

❸ How might people put the Sikh view about the role of the community into practice in their own lives?

Sikh beliefs about God

In this section you will:

- learn what Sikhs believe about God
- learn about the Mool Mantar
- consider how these beliefs might affect people's lives.

The Mool Mantar

One of the central statements of **Sikh** belief is in a short hymn called the **Mool Mantar**.

'Mool Mantar' means basic teaching, and is found at the beginning of the **Guru Granth Sahib Ji**. It is repeated each day during early morning prayer.

The first words of the Mool Mantar are **Ik Onkar**, meaning 'There is only One God'.

The symbol for Ik Onkar is seen in many places such as badges, on the walls of a **gurdwara** and in the home. It is a constant reminder to Sikhs of their faith and belief in **Waheguru**.

The Mool Mantar is a key statement of Sikh beliefs

Beliefs about God

The most important belief in Sikhism is that there is only one God – Waheguru. God is beyond the understanding of human beings. God cannot be described, because humans can only describe in human terms which will always be less than what God is. God is neither male nor female. God is the creator who created the world for people to use and enjoy. God is everywhere and beyond everything. However, God created people, and made them so that they would know the difference between right and wrong. Although people know the difference between right and wrong, they still have to choose for themselves which path they will follow. God is present in everyone's soul, but can only be seen by those who are blessed. God is personal and is available to everyone.

The Mool Mantar

Ik Onkar	There is only One God
Sat Nam	Eternal truth is God's name
Karta Purakh	God is the creator
Nir Bhau	God is without fear
Nir Vair	God is without hate
Akal Murat	Immortal, without form
Ajuni	Beyond birth and death
Saibhang	God is the enlightener
Gur Parshad	God can be reached through the mercy and grace of the true **Guru**

Sikhs believe that the one God is the God of all religions. No one religion can claim to be the only true way to God, and different religions are just different ways towards God. Therefore, it is not important which God people worship. What is important is that they follow God's teachings so that they have the chance of achieving **mukti**, or escape from rebirth.

You are Father, Mother, Friend, Brother, with you as support everywhere, what fear can I have?

Guru Granth Sahib Ji

> There are many names for God such as:
>
> | | |
> |---|---|
> | Sat Nam | Eternal Reality |
> | Akal Purakh | Eternal One |
> | Waheguru | Wonderful Lord |

One important Sikh belief is that Sikhs should keep the name of God in their minds and live their lives as God would wish. To do this, many Sikhs practise **Nam Japna** throughout the day by repeating the word 'Waheguru' under their breath.

Learning about religion

1   **a**   What is the Mool Mantar?

     b   Explain why this prayer is so important?

2   **a**   What does the Mool Mantar say about God?

     b   Why is this passage from the Guru Granth Sahib Ji important in what it teaches about God?

3   Consider what Sikhs mean when they say that there is only one God for all religions.

Learning from religion

1   **a**   What can we learn about God from Sikh teaching?

     b   In what ways might this belief help other people?

2   Explain why it might be important to think about God in our daily lives.

3   Think about how you might try to describe God.

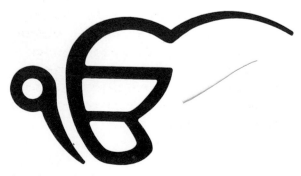

Ik Onkar – the first words of the Mool Mantar

Sikh beliefs about life

In this section you will:

● learn what Sikhs believe about how they should live their lives

● find out about mukti

● consider how these beliefs might affect people's lives.

Sikhs believe that everything that happens is **Hukam**, the will of God.

They belive that there is a divine spark – a part of God – in each person and this spark, or soul, is taken back to God when a person reaches **mukti** and is finally released from the cycle of rebirth.

Sikhs believe that there are nearly eight and a half million different forms of life, and that many souls have to travel though a large number of these before they can finally reach God – **Waheguru**. Each time something dies, the soul is reborn. It is only humans who can know the difference between right and wrong, and so it is only when the soul is in a human being that the cycle can be broken.

Sikhs believe that the ten **Gurus** had already reached a stage in life where they did not need to be reborn, but that they were sent back to earth to become God's messengers and lead other people to Waheguru.

Karma – actions and the consequences of these actions – decide whether a soul can be set free from the cycle. Freedom from this cycle is called mukti.

There are several things, or influences, that can stop a soul reaching mukti:

● a hankar – pride

● kam – lust or desire

● karodh – anger

● lobh – greed

Prayer is an important element of Sikh worship

Sikhs believe in hard work and helping others

- moh – being too attached to the world
- **manmukh** – being self-centred instead of God-centred (**gurmukh)**
- maya – delusion, that is, looking at the world and ignoring God.

Those who live without these influences, or dangers, devote their life to **sewa** – selfless service to others.

In order to avoid these dangers Sikhs are encouraged to follow rules of conduct.

- There is only one God. Worship and pray to God alone, and remember God at all times.
- Always work hard, and share with others.
- Live a truthful life.
- Remember that men and women are equal in God's eyes.
- The whole human race is one. Distinctions of **caste**, colour, class and religion are wrong.

- Idols, magic, omens, fasts, marks on the face and sacred threads are banned.
- Dress simply and modestly.
- **Khalsa** Sikh women should not wear the veil. Neither women nor men should make holes in their ears and noses.
- Live a married life.
- Put your faith in the **Guru Granth Sahib Ji.**
- Avoid lust, anger, greed, attachment to worldly things and arrogance.
- Live a humble and simple life.

Learning about religion

❶ **a** What is Hukam?

　b What do Sikhs mean by karma?

❷ **a** Explain why mukti is so important?

　b Explain what can stop a soul from reaching mukti.

❸ Consider and then write down how Sikhs are told to live their lives.

Learning from religion

❶ **a** What can we learn about a way of life from Sikh teaching?

　b In what ways might this belief help other people?

❷ Explain why it might be important to have a code of conduct.

❸ What rules of conduct would you include if you were making a set to live by?

Signs and symbols 1

Kara

Symbols are a way in which we remind ourselves, and other people, of important ideas and beliefs. Signs and symbols are used in everyday life, and many religions have particular symbols of their own.

There are a number of important symbols in Sikhism.

The five Ks

Sikhs who are members of the **Khalsa** (the community of the pure) are required to wear five symbols: **kara**, **kangha**, **kesh**, **kachera** and **kirpan**. These **five Ks**, or **panj kakke**, show that the person is a Sikh. They also have spiritual meanings and are symbols of the faith. They have their origins in the establishment of the Khalsa by **Guru** Gobind Singh Ji at **Baisakhi** in 1699, and they remind Sikhs of their beliefs and their history.

Kara

The kara is a bracelet, made of iron or steel, never silver or gold, which is worn on the right wrist. Some Sikhs wear two karas. The metal is a symbol of strength, and the circle is a symbol of unity and eternity because a circle has no beginning and no end. This symbolizes the Sikh view of God who is believed to be eternal and infinite. The circular shape also stands for the unity between Sikhs and between Sikhs and God. In the past, a wider version of the kara

was worn to protect the warrior's sword arm during a battle.

Kangha

The kangha is a comb used by Sikhs to keep their hair clean and tidy. When Guru Gobind Singh Ji founded the Khalsa he emphasized the importance of cleanliness. Sikhs are therefore encouraged to wash their hair early each morning. They then comb it and wind it into a topknot. The kangha is placed in the topknot to keep it in place. Sometimes the kangha has a small image of a **kirpan** (sword) on it. Using the khanga to keep their hair in place also reminds Sikhs of the need for discipline in order to live according to God's will.

Kangha

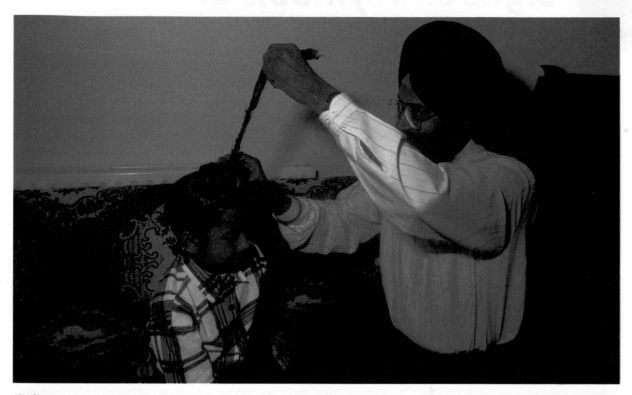

Kesh

Kesh

Kesh is uncut hair. Guru Gobind Singh Ji told Khalsa Sikhs not to cut their hair.

It should be allowed to grow as God intended it to. Many Sikh men keep their hair covered with a **turban**. Young boys whose hair has not yet grown long enough for a turban may wear a small cloth over their topknot to keep their hair clean.

Learning about religion

❶ What is meant by the panj kakke? Explain why they are so important to Sikhs.

❷ What is a kara? Explain why this is an important symbol for Sikhs.

❸ **a** What is special about kesh?

b Why do you think Sikhs insist on their right to wear a turban?

❹ Search the Internet to find information about occasions when Sikhs have not been allowed to wear their turbans in Britain (try www.sikhism.org.uk/main.htm to begin with). Write a summary about what you find out.

Learning from religion

❶ What can we learn about a way of life from the wearing of the five Ks?

❷ What other faith symbols can you think of? Do you think it might help people to wear symbols of their faith?

❸ What symbols would you like to wear to say something about your way of life and beliefs?

Signs and symbols 2

In this section you will:

● learn about the kachera, the kirpan and other Sikh symbols

● learn about the importance of these symbols

● consider how symbols are used in Sikhism and what can be learnt from this.

Kachera

Kachera are short trousers that are usually worn as undergarments. They are worn by men and women. **Guru** Gobind Singh Ji said that **Sikhs** should wear these short trousers as part of the **Khalsa** uniform. This may originally have been to distinguish Sikhs from Hindus, who traditionally wore dhotis (long loin cloths) or long cloaks. Both of these Hindu garments were unsuitable for fighting in and the kachera may have made it easier for Sikhs to fight in a battle if they had to do so.

Wearing these clothes reminds Sikhs that they must always be prepared to defend their religion and the rights of other people to practise their own faith. Today, these short trousers are seen as a symbol of modesty for many Sikhs and remind them of the need to live a good life according to the teachings of the Gurus.

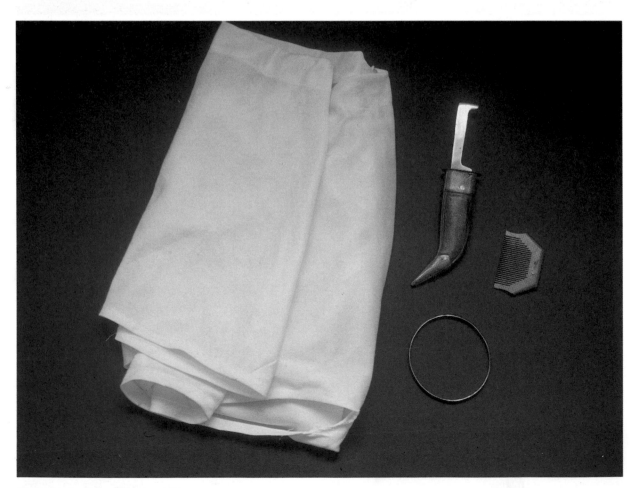

Kachera, kangha, kara and kirpan

Kirpan

The **kirpan** is a sword worn by members of the Khalsa. The kirpan is worn as a reminder of the courage of the first five Sikhs, the **panj piare**, who were willing to let Guru Gobind Singh Ji cut off their heads with a kirpan for the sake of their religion. So it is a symbol of bravery and of faith in God. There was a time, however, when Sikhs were persecuted by the Mogul emperors and when they had to be ready to defend not only themselves, but also their faith. The kirpan is worn as a symbol of the Sikh being willing to defend his or her faith, or to defend the weak or oppressed.

Taking the kirpan out of its sheath would be considered disrespectful by some Sikhs. The kirpan is worn on a belt, which goes across the shoulder under a coat. Because the kirpan is seen as a weapon, Sikhs outside of the Punjab have sometimes been told that they are not allowed to wear it in public. They have objected to the kirpan being called a dagger or a knife because this suggests that they are carrying it as a weapon. Sometimes the kirpan is worn as a very small symbol on the **kangha**.

Nishan Sahib

The Sikh flag and symbol is called the **Nishan Sahib**. This flag always flies outside a **gurdwara**. It is a triangle of saffron or orange cloth. On the flag is the **khanda**. The khanda itself has three important symbols on it. The first is a double-edged sword (also known as a khanda), which is used to stir **amrit** in gurdwara services. The second is the **kara** (circular bangle), given to Sikhs as a symbol of their unity and oneness with God. The third is two kirpans. The two kirpans represent spiritual power and worldly power, and were first carried by Guru Har Gobind Ji.

The flag is treated with great respect and is renewed each year at the festival of **Baisakhi**.

Ik Onkar

The first words of the **Mool Mantar** are **Ik Onkar**, meaning 'There is only One God'. The symbol for Ik Onkar (see page 17) is seen in many places, such as on badges, on the walls of a gurdwara and in the home. It is there as a constant reminder to Sikhs of their belief in one God – **Waheguru**.

Learning about religion

❶ **a** What is special about the kirpan?

b Why do you think Sikhs do not like the kirpan being called a dagger or a knife.

❷ Search the Internet for information about the five Ks (try www.sikhism.org.uk/main.htm to begin with). Write a report about what you find.

Learning from religion

❶ **a** What symbol might you use in your home in the same way as the Ik Onkar is used?

b Why do you think it would be helpful to have a symbol like this?

❷ What important symbols can you think of in daily life?

❸ Why is it sometimes easier to say something using symbols rather than words?

The gurdwara

In this section you will:

● learn about the gurdwara

● learn about the importance of these buildings

● consider how worship in a gurdwara might affect people's lives.

Gurdwara means 'the doorway of the **Guru**'. It is a building in which the **Sikh** holy book, the **Guru Granth Sahib Ji**, is kept, and it is a place where Sikhs worship together. A gurdwara is also a community centre for Sikhs where they have the opportunity to meet other Sikhs and also to worship together.

Gurdwaras are particularly important in Sikh communities outside of the Punjab, because in countries such as Britain, Sikhs may not live close to other Sikh families.

Outside a gurdwara there are usually symbols to show what it is. There is a flagpole flying the **Nishan Sahib**, the Sikh flag. This is triangular, orange or saffron in colour, and on it is a symbol known as the **khanda**. This consists of two curved **kirpans** (swords), a khanda (double-edged sword) and a **kara** (circular bangle).

Shoes must not be worn in the main prayer hall of a gurdwara. There are also sinks so that people can wash their hands before worship, and a box of head coverings for non-Khalsa Sikhs, because people must cover their heads as a sign of respect. Anyone is welcome in a gurdwara as long as they have no traces of alcohol or tobacco on them.

In the main prayer hall there is a large carpeted area. There are no seats or chairs because the **sadhsangat** (congregation) sit on the floor cross-legged. Feet must not point towards the Guru Granth Sahib Ji. Women and men sit on opposite sides of the gurdwara in order not to distract each other during worship.

Sikhs in a gurdwara, the central place of Sikh community worship

of explanation. Shabads are sung solemnly and slowly, and great care is taken to pronounce the words so that everyone can hear them clearly.

Inside a gurdwara there is a room that is the rest room for the holy scriptures. The rest room has a bed, with pillows, covers and a canopy. The Guru Granth Sahib Ji is 'put to bed' each night by the granthi or by another Sikh who says the **Kirtan Sohila** prayer. Each morning it is 'woken up' and placed on the manji.

The Guru Granth Sahib Ji is laid to rest for the night

At one end of the hall is the **manji** or sahib (a raised platform) with a **chanani** (canopy). There are cushions on the manji with **romalla** (beautiful cloths) draped over them. The romalla cover the Guru Granth Sahib Ji when it is not being read. This is the daytime resting place of the Guru Granth Sahib Ji. The **granthi**, who may be a man or a woman, sits behind the Guru Granth Sahib Ji, facing the worshippers.

In front of the manji there is a long box called a **golak**, in which worshippers place their money offerings.

There is another platform where the **ragis** (musicians) sit to play their instruments during **kirtan** (hymn singing). Music is an important aspect of Sikh worship as an accompaniment to the singing of the scriptures. Verses from the scriptures are set to music and are called **shabads**. The singing of shabads is called kirtan. The hymns found in the Guru Granth Sahib Ji are known as **Gurbani**, which means 'the words of the Guru'.

It is important for Sikhs to remember the words of the shabads, but it is more important that they understand their meaning. Before a hymn is sung, the ragis will read it and will say a few words

Learning about religion

1 **a** In your notes, write down the main features of a gurdwara.

 b What is the importance of the sinks and the box of head coverings?

 c Explain how people sit in a gurdwara.

2 Explain the symbols on the Nishan Sahib.

3 Why do you think it is so important for Sikhs to understand the shabads?

Learning from religion

1 **a** What might people learn about respect from the way in which Sikhs prepare to enter the prayer hall?

 b List the benefits and drawbacks of men and women sitting together to pray.

2 What do you think would be a helpful way for people to prepare themselves for worship?

3 What might people learn about worship from seeing Sikhs in a gurdwara?

The langar

In this section you will:

- learn about the langar
- learn about importance of sharing and equality in Sikhism
- consider how sharing food in a langar might affect people's lives.

Every **gurdwara** has a **langar** – 'Guru's kitchen' or eating area. The communal meal eaten here is also called a langar. The langar is part of the act of worship and is a very important aspect of **Sikh** life. There is no charge for the food served in the langar.

Guru Nanak Dev Ji started the custom of the langar because he rejected the Hindu **caste** system. In this system, people of different castes are not allowed to eat together. Guru Nanak Dev Ji

wanted to stress the idea that everyone is equal, so he wanted everyone to be able to eat the same food in the langar regardless of social class, sex, religion or caste. Also, everyone was to share the tasks of preparation, cooking, serving and cleaning. This shows **sewa** – selfless service to others in the **sadhsangat**, the gurdwara and the world outside. Sewa is a very important aspect of Sikhism.

This teaching was continued by Guru Amar Das Ji who made a rule that no one could see him until they had first eaten in the langar.

Sikh families consider it a privilege to provide for the langar and to serve others. There is usually a waiting list of people who want to provide the langar each week.

The food is usually served by the male members of the congregation. There are no special places and everyone eats the same food. Although not all Sikhs are vegetarian, no meat is served in the

Sharing food together in the langar illustrates the equality of all people before God

Vegetarian food is served in the langar so as not to exclude anyone

langar so that no one will be excluded from the meal regardless of their religion. Sikhs are not allowed to eat any meat that has been ritually slaughtered, such as that for Jews or Muslims.

Food is usually served on trays that have five or six compartments. These will probably contain food such as: chapatis, a vegetable curry, mixed salad, sweet rice or other sweet milk dishes, and pieces of fresh fruit.

Learning about religion

1 a What is meant by the word 'langar'? You should be able to think of several meanings.

b Explain Guru Nanak Dev Ji's teaching about the langar.

2 a Why do you think Guru Amar Das Ji refused to see anyone until they had eaten in the langar?

b Explain the arrangements for preparing and serving food in the langar.

3 Why do you think the langar is still so important to Sikhism?

Learning from religion

1 a What might people learn from eating in a langar?

b Why might other people set up places like the langar?

2 Sex, social class, colour and religion are some of the ways in which people discriminate against others. Think of examples of ways in which people suffer as a result of such forms of discrimination, and write about them.

3 What might people learn about equality from the idea of the langar?

Worship 1

In this section you will:

- learn about the Sikh service of worship
- learn about importance of this worship
- consider how this type of regular worship might affect people's lives.

There is no fixed day for worship in Sikhism, although Sunday is a popular day both in India and other countries. This is because it is a day when most people do not go to work. Some communities have their services daily, or in the evenings.

Prayers are said every morning and evening in the **gurdwara**, but not all members of the local community attend these.

Congregational worship is called **diwan**, but this service is sometimes called **kirtan**. 'Kirtan' means hymn-singing, because verses from the **Guru Granth Sahib Ji** are sung as part of the service.

The weekly service

After bathing, members of the **sadhsangat** remove their shoes, cover their heads and wash their hands before entering the prayer hall.

As they enter the prayer hall, **Sikhs** approach the **manji** or sahib (platform) on which the Guru Granth Sahib Ji is placed. They kneel on their hands and knees, and lower their heads until their foreheads touch the floor as a sign of respect.

Then they make an offering of money, flowers or food for the use of the Sikh community.

Sikhs may then greet other members of the congregation by saying **Waheguru** before taking up their places, sitting cross-legged on the floor facing the manji. It is traditional for men and women to sit on opposite sides of the prayer hall.

The service may last for two hours or more. It begins early in the morning when the Guru Granth Sahib Ji is removed from its resting place and placed on the manji. There are readings

Sikhs kneeling in front of the Guru Granth Sahib Ji

The Ardas is an important Sikh prayer

from the Guru Granth Sahib Ji until the **ragis** (musicians) arrive. The readings are chosen at random.

People chant verses from the Guru Granth Sahib Ji, and the ragis sing and accompany them on musical Instruments. The congregation joins in some of the hymns. This part of the service is called kirtan.

Near to the end of the service, a sermon is given by a member of the Sikh community. This is usually an explanation of the readings from the Guru Granth Sahib Ji.

At the end of the service there is a series of prayers, which includes: six verses from the **Anand Sahib**, a hymn written by Guru Amar Das Ji, the last part of the **Japji Sahib**, written by **Guru Nanak Dev Ji**, a verse from a hymn by Guru Arjan Dev Ji, and, finally, **Ardas**.

When Ardas is said, members of the congregation stand and face the Guru Granth Sahib Ji with the palms of their hands together as a mark of respect.

The first part of Ardas mentions God and all the Gurus. The second part reminds Sikhs that the Guru Granth Sahib Ji is God's word, and of the faithful Sikhs of the past. The final part of Ardas is a prayer asking God to keep the **Khalsa** faithful and for the well-being of people of all races and religions.

While Ardas is being said, someone in the congregation prepares the **karah parshad** (a sweet food that is shared by the congregation) by stirring it with a **kirpan**. After Ardas, everyone sits down. The karah parshad is offered first to five practising Sikhs, in memory of the **panj piare**, and then handed out to everyone present. The karah parshad is placed in people's hands. This shared food shows that everyone is equal before God.

Learning about religion

1 **a** When is the Sikh weekly service of worship usually held?

b Explain what Sikhs do when they enter the gurdwara.

2 **a** What is the importance of the offerings that Sikhs make in the prayer hall?

b What is special about Ardas?

3 How is respect shown to the Guru Granth Sahib Ji during the service?

Learning from religion

1 **a** What can we learn about worship from a Sikh service?

b How do you think it might help non-religious people if they were to learn about and show respect for holy books?

2 Find out how some other religions treat their holy books and why.

3 Explain the importance of the teaching in the final part of Ardas and suggest how other people might learn from this.

Worship 2

In this section you will:
- learn about Sikh daily worship
- learn about the importance of this worship
- consider how this type of regular worship might affect people's lives.

Nam Simran

Guru Nanak Dev Ji taught that the most important form of worship is **bhakti** (devotion to God). Some people say that the whole of Sikhism is bhakti.

When **Sikhs** meditate on the name of God, this is known as **Nam Simran** (thinking of the name). In this way, people sense God within themselves and grow ever closer to God.

Sikhs remember the presence of God through **Nam Japna**, a constant repetition of the name of God, '**Waheguru**'. This can be said aloud or silently.

Morning prayer

After bathing, meditate upon the Lord and your body and mind will become pure.

Guru Granth Sahib Ji

Guru Ram Das Ji said:

He who calls himself a Sikh of the great Sat Guru should rise early and meditate on God's name.

Guru Granth Sahib Ji

Mala – prayer beads

Sikhs get up early each day to pray and to meditate. This is called **amritvela**. The early morning is peaceful and is a good time for prayer and meditation. First, they take a bath and get dressed, then after covering their heads, they can begin prayer.

Prayer begins with the **Japji Sahib**, a hymn of 38 verses which comes from the first section of the **Guru Granth Sahib Ji**. The opening verses of the Japji Sahib are the **Mool Mantar**. After the Japji Sahib, other prayers are said and, if there is time, some Sikhs will read hymns from a collection called the **gutka**. At the end of prayers, Sikhs meditate. Some people use **mala** (prayer beads) to help them.

Sikhs do not have set prayer positions. Prayers must not be said while doing other things and, ideally, should be done in a quiet place without any distractions.

Throughout the day, some Sikhs will often practise Nam Japna by repeating the word 'Waheguru', usually under their breath.

Sikh women praying at home

Evening prayer

In the evening, there are set hymns and prayers. **Sodar Rahiras** is said before the evening meal. Just before going to bed, Sikhs will recite a small group of hymns called the **Kirtan Sohila**.

Learning about religion

❶ a In your notes, write down what is meant by bhakti.

b Explain what is meant by Nam Simran.

❷ a Why are the two quotations from the Guru Granth Sahib Ji important when thinking about Sikh prayer?

b What conditions are important for prayer?

❸ How do Sikhs pray in the evening?

Learning from religion

❶ a What can we learn about prayer from the daily prayers of Sikhs?

b Do you think it might help all people if they were to pray more regularly? Would it help you? Explain your views.

❷ Find out about different ways in which people meditate.

❸ What might people learn from the Sikh practice of washing before prayers?

The Guru Granth Sahib Ji

In this section you will:

● learn about the Guru Granth Sahib Ji

● learn about respect shown to the Guru Granth Sahib Ji

● consider how showing this respect might affect people's lives.

The **Guru Granth Sahib Ji** is the holy scriptures of the **Sikhs**. The book is written in Punjabi, using the **Gurmukhi** – 'from the mouth of the **Guru**' – script. Every printed copy of the Guru Granth Sahib Ji is exactly the same, with 1430 pages. The Guru Granth Sahib Ji can be translated, but these translations are not used in Sikh worship.

The Guru Granth Sahib Ji is a collection of the teachings and hymns of **Guru Nanak Dev Ji** and five of the other Sikh Gurus. It is treated as a living Guru by Sikhs, as Guru Gobind Singh Ji instructed.

The second Guru, Guru Angad Dev Ji, wrote down the hymns of Guru Nanak Dev Ji. The third Guru, Guru Amar Das Ji, composed more hymns, including the **Anand Sahib** (Hymn of Bliss). The fourth Guru, Guru Ram Das Ji, composed the **Lavan**, the four verses that are sung at a wedding ceremony while the bride and groom are walking around the holy book. The fifth Guru, Guru Arjan Dev Ji, brought all the hymns of the other Gurus into one single set of scriptures, known as the **Adi Granth**.

Guru Gobind Singh Ji added more hymns written by his father, Guru Tegh Bahadur Ji. He announced that, after his death, there would be no other living Guru, but that the scriptures should now become the Guru.

Reading from the Guru Granth Sahib Ji

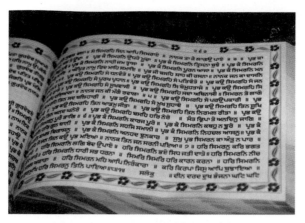

A page of the Guru Granth Sahib Ji, written in Gurmukhi script

The Adi Granth then became a 'Guru', and was known as the Guru Granth Sahib Ji.

The Guru Granth Sahib Ji is given the same respect that was shown to the human Gurus during their lifetimes. It has a special resting place where it is put to bed every evening.

At the beginning of each day, the **granthi**, and any other Sikhs present, form a procession to carry the Guru Granth Sahib Ji to its position in the main prayer hall of the **gurdwara** on the **manji**.

The Guru Granth Sahib Ji is never placed on the ground and Sikhs never turn their backs on it.

While the Guru Granth Sahib Ji is being read, the granthi waves a special fan, called a **chauri**, over the pages of the book. This chauri has a long handle and is made from yak's hair. It is used in remembrance of a **pakha**, which was used by Sikhs walking with the Gurus to keep them cool in the hot areas of the Punjab.

The Guru Granth Sahib Ji is of very great importance for Sikhs, who believe that its message is **Gurbani** – the word of God.

Many Sikhs own a copy of the Guru Granth Sahib Ji and take care to show it respect. Some Sikh families have a copy of the **Dasam Granth**, poetry written by Guru Gobind Singh Ji and not included in the Guru Granth Sahib Ji or the sacred **Nit nem** (a prayer book) at home.

Learning about religion

❶ a What is meant by the word 'Gurmukhi'?

b Explain how the Guru Granth Sahib Ji came into being.

❷ a Why do you think the use of the chauri is important?

b Explain how the Guru Granth Sahib Ji is shown respect in the gurdwara and at home.

❸ Find out how holy books are treated by members of other religions.

Learning from religion

❶ What might people learn from the respect that Sikhs show to the Guru Granth Sahib Ji?

❷ Consider the importance of thinking about a book as being the actual words of God.

❸ What things do some people show the same respect to in their lives as Sikhs show to the Guru Granth Sahib Ji?

Festivals 1

In this section you will:

● learn about some of the Sikh festivals

● learn about how these festivals are celebrated

● consider how celebrating these festivals might affect people's lives.

There are two different types of festivals in Sikhism.

1 Special holy days, which celebrate events in the lives of the **Gurus**. These are known as **gurpurbs** – Gurus' remembrance days.

2 Other celebrations, which are held on the same days as some Hindu festivals. These are known as **melas**.

Sikhs also celebrate the anniversaries of great events in Sikh history, such as **Baisakhi**, the foundation of the **Khalsa** in 1699.

Gurpurbs

The gurpurbs are days that remember the births and deaths of the Gurus. Some of these are particularly important. The dates are usually set according to the Indian calendar, but, in recent years, most of them have been placed on fixed dates. They include:

● the martyrdom of Guru Arjan Dev Ji (May/June) (16 June)

● the installation of the **Guru Granth Sahib Ji** (August/early September)

● the birthday of **Guru Nanak Dev Ji** (November)

● the birthday of Guru Gobind Singh Ji (December) (5 January)

● the martyrdom of Guru Tegh Bahadur Ji (December) (24 November).

Part of the celebration of a gurpurb is a complete reading of the Guru Granth Sahib Ji.

The Guru Granth Sahib Ji being carried through the streets at a gurpurb

Sikhs celebrating the birthday of Guru Nanak Dev Ji

This is called the **Akhand Path**. Sikhs usually come to the **gurdwara** on the last day of the Akhand Path to hear the last pages of the Guru Granth Sahib Ji being read.

In India, these events are celebrated on the actual day on which they fall, but in other countries, where Sikh communities are smaller, they are usually celebrated on the closest Sunday. The Akhand Path begins on Friday and ends at the Sunday service.

In India, the Guru Granth Sahib Ji is traditionally carried through the streets in a procession with five men representing the **panj piare**.

Learning about religion

❶ What is a gurpurb? Why are some days celebrated as gurpurbs?

❷ **a** What is the Akhand Path?

b Explain how observing the Akhand Path is a sign of great respect to the Gurus.

❸ Visit The Sikhism Homepage on the Internet (www.sikhs.org) and find out more about the celebration of gurpurbs. (You could also try http://theresite.org.uk)

Learning from religion

❶ **a** What might people learn from the way in which Sikhs celebrate gurpurbs?

b Consider how people celebrate the anniversaries of deaths and births in their families.

❷ 'Although it's a good idea to celebrate birthdays, it is strange to celebrate someone's death.' Explain your views on this statement.

❸ Do you think that reading a holy book as Sikhs do during the Akhand Path might be a good way to celebrate festivals?

Festivals 2

In this section you will:

● learn about more of the Sikh festivals

● learn about how these festivals are celebrated

● consider how celebrating these festivals might affect people's lives.

Mela

There are three major **Sikh** festivals that are held on the same day as Hindu festivals. They are:

● **Baisakhi**

● **Divali Mela**

● **Hola Mohalla Mela**.

The word '**mela**' means 'a fair'.

Guru Amar Das Ji said that Sikhs should come together for worship during Baisakhi and Divali Mela. Guru Gobind Singh Ji added Hola Mohalla Mela as another time when Sikhs should celebrate together. Celebrating these festivals together confirmed that Sikhs were a separate religious group and that they no longer celebrated the festivals as Hindus.

Baisakhi

Baisakhi is the month of the wheat harvest in the Punjab. The festival is on 13 April (on 14 April once every 36 years), and now marks the Sikh New Year.

In 1699, Guru Gobind Singh Ji founded the **Khalsa** at Baisakhi. Sikhs also remember 1919, when 400 Sikhs (many of them women and children) were killed by British soldiers who had been ordered to break up their Baisakhi gathering at Jallianwala Bagh in **Amritsar**.

Changing the Nishan Sahib at Baisakhi

The **Nishan Sahib**, the Sikh flag, is changed at Baisakhi. During the festival, the **Akhand Path** is read and initiation ceremonies (**amrit**) are held.

In Amritsar, Baisakhi is a great animal fair. In India, many Sikhs are farmers, so a livestock market is not unusual.

Because Baisakhi is associated with the idea of forming a Sikh nation, there are often political speeches at this festival.

Divali Mela

Divali Mela is celebrated throughout India in the autumn, and marks the end of the rainy season.

Sikhs remember the story of Guru Har Gobind Ji who returned to Amritsar on Divali. He had been in prison while the Mogul Emperor tried to stop the growth of Sikhism. The Emperor was sick, and his doctors said that his illness was caused because he had imprisoned a man of God. Guru Har Gobind Ji was released, but he said that he would not go unless he could take 52 Hindu princes who were also in prison with him.

The Mogul Jehangir told the Guru that he would free as many princes as could hold on to his clothes as he walked through a narrow passage.

The Golden Temple during Divali Mela

Guru Har Gobind Ji made himself a coat with long tassels, and all the princes went with him.

Many Sikh homes are decorated with divas (clay lamps), candles and coloured lights. There are special meals and firework displays. It is a time of rejoicing. People give sweets to their friends and relatives. Services are held in **gurdwaras**, and the Golden Temple in Amritsar is lit up.

Hola Mohalla Mela

In 1700, Guru Gobind Singh Ji held a three-day festival at **Anandpur**. This became a time for Sikhs to train as soldiers. Guru Gobind Singh Ji wanted to prepare them for any trouble that might come.

Hola Mohalla means 'attack and counter-attack'.

Learning about religion

❶ a What is a mela?

  b Explain why Guru Amar Das Ji wanted Sikhs to come together at these festivals.

❷ What is remembered at Baisakhi? In your own words, describe the escape of Guru Har Gobind Ji. Explain which of these three festivals you think is the most important, and say why.

Learning from religion

❶ What might people learn from the way in which Sikhs celebrate the melas?

❷ Find out more about what happened at Jallianwala Bagh in 1919. You could use the Internet to help you. Try doing a search for Jallianwala Bagh.

❸ Explain why festivals play such an important part in all religions.

❹ How might people today follow the example of Guru Har Gobind Ji?

Pilgrimage 1

In this section you will:
- learn about pilgrimage
- learn about some of the places that Sikhs might visit
- consider how pilgrimage might affect people's lives.

There are no special times for pilgrimage in Sikhism, but many **Sikhs** try to visit places associated with their religion. Sikhs believe that God is everywhere, and so no one place is more holy than another.

The **Gurus** taught that it was not important to make special journeys to visit holy places. The important aspect of Sikh life is living according to God's will.

True pilgrimage consists of the contemplation of the name of God and the cultivation of inner knowledge.

Guru Granth Sahib Ji

There is no place of pilgrimage equal to the Gurus. The Guru alone is the pool of contentment. The Guru is the river from which pure water is obtained, by which the dirt of evil understanding is washed away.

Guru Granth Sahib Ji

The Punjab in India is the homeland of Sikhs. More than half of the people who live there are Sikhs, and the language they speak is Punjabi. Of the world population of more than 19 million Sikhs, 80 per cent live in the Punjab. Sikhs who do not live in the Punjab may also visit the Golden Temple at **Amritsar** and other places associated with the Gurus and their lives. These visits are called **yatras**.

Harimandir Sahib – the Golden Temple – is a very important centre of pilgrimage for Sikhs

The Harimandir Sahib

The most popular place to go on a yatra is the **Harimandir Sahib** – the Golden Temple at Amritsar. 'Harimandir' means 'God's House', and '**Sahib**' is a word that is added to the names of people, places and things to show how much they are respected.

The Harimandir Sahib is a very special **gurdwara**. The first Guru, **Guru Nanak Dev Ji**, chose the site, which he said was a place of great beauty, and he said that the fourth Guru would build there. Guru Ram Das Ji began to build a large pool there, which he filled with **amrit** (nectar) and named Amritsar. This sort of pool is called a **serovar**. His son, Guru Arjan Dev Ji, built the Harimandir Sahib on an island in the middle of the serovar, and this work was finished in 1601.

The Harimandir Sahib has always been a major meeting place for Sikhs when they have been persecuted. The Mogul emperors destroyed the temple and filled in the serovar. A Sikh leader, Baba Deep Singh, led a group of Sikhs who destroyed the Mogul army and restored the temple. In 1740 the temple was used as a hall for dancing and drinking. Two Sikhs travelled from the south of India to kill the ruler of Amritsar and to restore the temple.

The dome and the upper walls of the Harimandir Sahib are covered in gold leaf. There is a door on each of the four walls facing east, west, north and south, to show that the Harimandir Sahib is open to everyone. A long marble walkway crosses the serovar to the west door of the Harimandir Sahib, while a wide promenade, called the Pakirama, runs around the pool. There are also rows of rooms where pilgrims can rest. The **langar** in the Harimandir Sahib is open every day and anyone can eat there. The langar provides daily food for many of the poor people of Amritsar.

Learning about religion

1 a What is a yatra?

  b Explain why Sikhs might visit Amritsar.

2 a In your own words, describe the purpose of the Harimandir.

  b Explain how Sikhs have protected and care for the Harimandir.

3 Create a poster to show the most important features of the Harimandir. Search the Internet to find pictures, and annotate them to explain why they are significant.

Learning from religion

1 a What might people learn from the Sikh teaching that God is everywhere, and so no one place is more holy than another?

  b What might we learn from the example of Baba Deep Singh?

2 Why do you think so many people feel that making a pilgrimage is important?

3 Explain where you would like to go on a pilgrimage and why. How might the pilgrimage affect you?

Pilgrimage 2

Akal Takht

Akal Takht means 'the Throne of the Eternal'. The Akal Takht faces the Golden Temple – the **Harimandir Sahib** – and was built by **Guru** Har Gobind Ji in 1609. The building is used by **Sikhs** for political meetings and is the meeting place of the **Khalsa**. The highest Sikh court meets at the Akal Takht to make decisions on behalf of the whole Sikh community.

The Akal Takht is a central place for Sikh meetings

The building was destroyed by the Indian army in 1984, but has since been rebuilt.

The Akal Takht houses the most sacred copy of the **Guru Granth Sahib Ji**. Each day, at 5.00 am in winter and 4.00 am in summer, it is carried in a golden **palanquin** to the Harimandir. It is carried back to rest at 10.00 pm in winter and 11.00 pm in summer. Outside the building are two large flagpoles. One has the flag of Miri – earthly authority – and the other of Piri – spiritual authority.

Anandpur Sahib

Anandpur Sahib is another special place for Sikhs. It is in a valley at the foot of the Himalayas. The ashes of the head of Guru Tegh Bahadur Ji are buried there, and it is also the place where Guru Gobind Singh Ji founded the **Khalsa**. The most important celebrations for the festival of **Hola Mohalla Mela** take place at Anandpur.

Goindwal

Guru Amar Das Ji had a very deep well, or baoli, built at **Goindwal**. It provided safe drinking water and was surrounded by trees to improve the environment. It became a tradition for people to bathe in the well and, as people go down into it, they say the **Japji Sahib** on each of the 84 steps. Some people say that, by doing this, they will get nearer to **mukti**.

> Pilgrimage, austerity [living simply], mercy, almsgiving and charity bring merit, be it as little as a mustard seed, but those who hear, believe and cherish the word, an inner pilgrimage and cleansing is theirs.
>
> From the Japji Sahib

The Gurus said that ceremonial bathing served no purpose. When people recite the Japji Sahib going down into the well, they do not benefit from the bathing. They benefit because they have meditated on God's name.

If someone goes to bathe at a place of pilgrimage with the mind of a crook and the body of a thief then his outside will have been washed but his inside will be dirty twice over… The saints are good even without such washing. The thief remains a thief even if they bathe at a place of pilgrimage.

Guru Granth Sahib Ji

The entrance to the well at Goindwal

Learning about religion

❶ a In your own words, describe the Akal Takht.

b Explain why the Akal Takht is important for Sikhs.

❷ Explain why Sikhs might visit Anandpur Sahib.

❸ Explain the Gurus' teachings about pilgrimage and ritual bathing.

Learning from religion

❶ a What might people learn from the Sikh teaching that it is how you live that is important, not where you go or what you do there?

b The Akal Takht is a political, religious and community building. Do you think it would be a good idea if other religions brought these aspects of life together?

❷ Design a flag that contains what you believe to be important symbols.

❸ Find out about pilgrimage in other religions and explain which style of pilgrimage you might find most useful.

Growing up

Birth

As soon as a baby is born, many **Sikhs** whisper the words of the **Mool Mantar** in his or her ear and place a drop of honey on his or her tongue.

The name-giving ceremony

Once the mother and child are well enough to go out, there is a special ceremony held at the **gurdwara**. In the UK this usually happens during the regular weekly service.

The **granthi** opens the **Guru Granth Sahib Ji** at random. The baby's name will begin with the first letter of the first hymn on the left-hand side of the page. The parents are then given some time to choose a name. This name is announced by the granthi, who adds the title **Singh** for a boy or **Kaur** for a girl. The granthi then shouts 'Jo bole so nihal' ('Whoever believes in the truth will be saved'), and the **Sadhsangat**, or congregation, reply 'Sat sri akahl' ('The Truth is eternal').

The ceremony ends with the **Anand Sahib** (Hymn of Bliss), and **karah parshad** is given to the congregation.

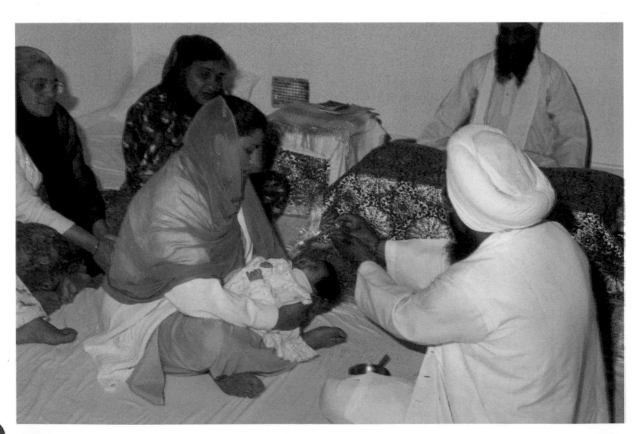

The name-giving ceremony is a special event which takes place in the gurdwara

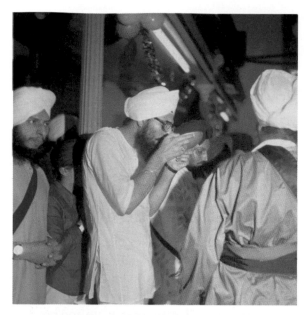

The Amrit ceremony is the initiation ceremony for Khalsa Sikhs

Initiation into the Khalsa

Boys and girls aged fourteen or sixteen are able to join the **Khalsa**. In order to join the Khalsa, Sikhs must have the **panj kakke** – the five Ks: **kesh** (uncut hair); **kangha** (a wooden comb); **kachera** (short trousers); **kirpan** (a short sword); and **kara** (an iron or steel bangle).

The ceremony is called the **Amrit** ceremony, and is conducted by five members of the Sikh community, who are already members of the Khalsa, representing the **panj piare**. They wear ceremonial robes: knee-length tunics in orange or saffron, blue sashes around their waists and over the shoulder, and a blue or orange turban.

One of the five members of the Khalsa explains the principles of the Sikh faith and reminds the candidates of the teachings of the Guru Granth Sahib Ji. The candidates for initiation are asked if they accept these principles. The five members of the Khalsa then kneel around an iron bowl, and prepare amrit from sugar and water. The bowl represents strength. The water represents the source of life. Sikhs believe that once this water has been blessed, it purifies the soul. The liquid is stirred with a **khanda** (a double-edged sword).

Hymns are sung from the Guru Granth Sahib Ji, the candidates drink amrit, and say these words: 'The Khalsa is of God, the victory is to God.' The amrit is sprinkled on the hair and eyes of the candidates five times, then the Mool Mantar is read and repeated. **Ardas** is said and karah parshad is distributed to everyone.

Sikhs who do not join the Khalsa are called **Sahaj-dhari** – 'seekers after God'.

Learning about religion

1 **a** What ceremonies take place when a Sikh baby is born?

b Why do you think these ceremonies take place?

2 **a** What are the conditions for being initiated into the Khalsa?

b Describe the Amrit ceremony.

3 Why might joining the Khalsa be so important for a Sikh?

Learning from religion

1 **a** Explain why it might be important for a baby to be introduced into a religion.

b Do you think that it is a good idea for all young children to be brought up within a religion? Explain your views.

2 Why do you think making a commitment to a religion when you are a teenager is important to many people?

3 Do you think it would be a good idea if all people had to make this sort of commitment when they are teenagers? Explain your views.

Marriage

In this section you will:

- learn about the Sikh marriage ceremony
- learn the Sikh teachings about the importance of marriage
- consider how marriage ceremonies affect people and why they are important.

Marriage is a very important part of Sikhism. Although some marriages are still arranged by the families of the bride and groom, the couple both have the right to reject the partner chosen for them. A marriage brings two families together and **Sikhs** believe it is important that the families can get on with each other. This is why Sikhs do not encourage people to marry outside of their religion.

There is sometimes an engagement ceremony in the **gurdwara**, where God is thanked for bringing the couple together. After this, the groom's mother visits the bride and gives her a gold ring to wear.

Anand karaj – the wedding ceremony

A Sikh wedding usually takes place in the morning and must be held in front of a copy of the **Guru Granth Sahib Ji**. In India, a bride may be dressed very traditionally in red, but elsewhere the bride may wear white and be dressed very simply. Her head will be covered with a chunni (scarf). The groom wears a coloured **turban** and scarf, and carries a **kirpan**.

Before the service begins there is a ceremony called the **Milna**. The two families meet and give gifts, then eat a meal.

A Sikh wedding in India

The Lavan ceremony in Britain

The ceremony begins with the morning hymn, **Asa di var**, and **Ardas**.

Any Sikh may conduct the ceremony. The first part is an explanation of the Sikh ideal of marriage and the fact that marriage is not just a social contract but the joining together of two souls.

The bride and groom both bow to the Guru Granth Sahib Ji, which shows that they accept these teachings and that they want to spend the rest of their lives together, supporting each other physically and spiritually.

The bride's father places flower garlands over the couple, then takes one end of the groom's scarf and ties it to the end of the bride's head scarf to show that she is leaving her father and joining her husband.

The **Lavan** (wedding hymn) of **Guru** Ram Das Ji is sung and after each of the four verses the couple walk clockwise around the Guru Granth Sahib Ji, the bride following the groom. Each time, they bow to the Guru Granth Sahib Ji to show that they accept the teachings of the Lavan. The Lavan explains the relationship between God and an individual, and the couple are reminded to follow this throughout their married life.

The service ends with the sharing of **karah parshad**.

Although the guests may give money to the couple, the idea of a dowry is forbidden in Sikhism.

Everyone eats a simple meal in the **langar** after the ceremony, and the bride and groom go to their new home together.

Sikhs are expected to remain faithful to their husband or wife. It is hoped that the couple will stay together for life, but Sikhs accept that divorce, although unwelcome, is sometimes inevitable. Widows and widowers are allowed to remarry in a gurdwara.

Learning about religion

1 **a** What is an 'arranged marriage'?

b Why might Sikhs discourage their children from marrying non-Sikhs?

2 **a** Describe the main features of the Anand karaj.

b Explain what happens during the Lavan.

3 Why do you think marriage is such an important aspect of Sikhism?

Learning from religion

1 **a** Explain why some people might think arranged marriages are a good idea while others may not.

b Explain why people might prefer to have a religious wedding ceremony rather than marry in a register office (a civil ceremony).

2 In what ways might a couple find that a religious ceremony helps them when they meet problems in their married life?

3 Write a short marriage ceremony, and explain the vows and promises you think people should make to each other.

Creation

In this section you will:

● learn about what Sikhs believe about the creation

● learn the importance of these beliefs

● consider how these beliefs might affect people and their attitudes.

Sikhism is based on the 'Oneness of Creation'. **Sikhs** believe that the universe was made by God who created the earth and all forms of life on it. God is in charge, and arranges the birth, life and death of everything.

Humans, trees, holy places
Coasts, clouds, fields
Islands, continents, universes
Spheres and solar systems
Life forms – egg-born, womb-born, earth-born, sweat-born

Only God knows their existence
in oceans, mountains, everywhere
Nanak says God created them
and God takes care of them all.

Guru Granth Sahib Ji

Sikhs believe that before the creation there was no earth, no sky, no sun and no life. Only God existed alone until God's decision to create the world. Then God created everything by a single word.

God is responsible for all of creation, and everything in and on the earth belongs to God. God is in charge of all life and without God's **Hukam** (will) nothing can exist, change or develop.

However, since creating the world God has cared for it – God looks after it and protects it. There is no single aspect of the earth that God does not care for and so, according to **Guru** Arjan Dev Ji:

Even creatures in rocks and stones are well provided for. Birds who fly thousands of miles away leaving their young ones behind know that they would be sustained and taught to fend for themselves by God.

Sikhs believe that all creatures lead their lives under God's rule.

If I were a doe living in the forest, eating grass and leaves, with God's Grace I will find God.
If I were a cuckoo living in the mango tree, contemplating
and singing, God reveals through God's mercy.

Guru Granth Sahib Ji

Sikhism teaches that God created five elements – air, water, earth, fire and space. Everything in nature and the environment is made from these elements. Water is the most important of the elements, but all the elements must be kept in balance to avoid disaster.

God created night and day, seasons, time and occasions. So also air, water, fire and nether regions. Amidst these has God fixed the earth, the place for Righteous Activities.

Guru Granth Sahib Ji

Learning about religion

❶ What do you think is meant by the 'Oneness of Creation'?

❷ **a** What does Sikhism teach about the relationship between God and the animals?

b Explain how God takes care of the world, according to Sikh teaching.

❸ Why do you think these beliefs about creation are important for Sikhs?

Learning from religion

❶ Many religions have stories about how the world was created. Why do you think this is? Do you think that it is important for a religion to have these stories?

❷ Does it matter if religious stories are true? Explain your views.

❸ Explain how you believe the world was created.

The environment

In this section you will:

- learn Sikh teachings about caring for the environment
- learn why these are important for Sikhs
- consider what people might learn from these teachings.

Sikhs believe that God created the world as a place where every type of plant and animal could live so that all life could have the chance to prove that it was good enough to reach **mukti**.

Guru Nanak Dev Ji taught that:

Nature we see
Nature we hear
Nature we observe with awe, wonder and joy
Nature in the nether regions
Nature in the skies

Nature in the whole creation
Nature in the sacred texts (Vedas, Puranas and Qur'an)
Nature in all reflection
Nature in food, in water, in garments and in love for all
Nature in species, kinds, colours
Nature in life forms
Nature in good deeds
Nature in pride and in ego
Nature in air, water and fire
Nature in the soil of the earth
All nature is yours, O powerful Creator
You command it, observe it and pervade within it.

Guru Granth Sahib Ji

Although Sikhs believe that humans are the stewards of the earth and have to look after it, they also believe that God's spirit is in everything. Therefore many Sikhs are vegetarians.

Causing damage to the environment is harmful, and so Sikhs believe they must take care not to disturb the balance of nature.

Working to save the environment

Oil pollution damages the environment

Pray to God – remember God and God's authority always;

Earn an honest living – do not take what does not belong to you, or more than you need – essential truths for a proper relationship with nature;

Share with others – this includes all creation, not just human beings.

Guru Granth Sahib Ji

In the Punjab, rainfall is vital and always welcomed. When the monsoon arrives Sikhs celebrate because God has been good to them.

The lives of the **Gurus** are full of stories of their love for nature. Therefore, Sikhs are forbidden to kill for the sake of killing or in order to eat to excess.

In Sikh hymns, God is said to be the provider of all life. There is no difference between the world of humans and the world of nature. Both are equally important and must be treated with respect.

The Gurus have strongly made us aware of our responsibility towards this earth.

Guru Granth Sahib Ji

Sikhs believe that the environment can only be preserved if the balance that God created is maintained. The principles for this are found in the Guru Granth Sahib Ji.

Learning about religion

1 a What is meant by 'the environment'?

b What is a steward?

2 Explain why Sikhs give thanks when the monsoon arrives.

3 Why are Sikhs forbidden to kill for fun or sport?

4 Why do you think the Sikh teaching about caring for the environment is important?

Learning from religion

1 a Why do you think people are so concerned about the environment?

b Do you think that people should be more concerned about the environment? Explain your views.

2 In what ways do Sikhs put their teachings about the environment into practice? How might non-Sikhs carry out some of these ideas?

3 'Other animals are just as important as human beings.' Consider this statement and explain why you agree or disagree with it.

Human rights

It is a very important teaching of Sikhism, both in the **Guru Granth Sahib Ji** and in everyday life, that everyone is equal regardless of race, sex, class, **caste** or religion. Any hungry person who visits a **gurdwara** will always be fed.

A Hindu Brahmin. Guru Nanak Dev Ji taught that the caste system was wrong

Sikhs believe that God, who is the creator and source of all forms of life, is without any form, sex or colour. Therefore, any differences that are visible between humans whom God created are irrelevant – they do not make any one person better than any other. Any act of kindness that is performed towards another human being is an act of respect towards creation and is seen as an act of worship to God.

Guru Nanak Dev Ji was born a Hindu, and Sikhism has kept some of the teachings of Hinduism. For example, Hinduism also welcomes people of all religious beliefs. However, Guru Nanak Dev Ji taught that the caste system of Hinduism was wrong.

There are four varnas (castes), which form divisions within Hindu society. Within these varnas, there are also many jati (caste groups). Hindus believe that every Hindu is born into a particular caste because of their behaviour in a previous life, and that these castes cannot be changed. The first and highest caste is the Brahmin (teacher or priest), the second is the Kshatriya (ruler or warrior), the third is the Vaishya (merchant or farmer) and the fourth is the Shudra (servant or labourer).

People who are born below any of these castes are thought of as untouchables or outcasts, and are sometimes called dalit (oppressed). The caste system affects almost everything a Hindu does. Marriages should only take place between members of the same caste. Some Hindus will not eat with, or take food from, members of castes lower than theirs.

When Guru Nanak Dev Ji founded Sikhism, he intended that the discrimination of the caste system would be abolished. Unfortunately, some people still believe that it is important and it can sometimes influence aspects of Sikh life such as marriage, where members of one group may be unwilling to marry a member of another.

However, Sikhs are taught to treat all people equally and hope to be treated the same.

The langar is a place where Sikhs can offer hospitality to all

A Sikh independent homeland

One of the major problems for Sikhs today in seeking equality is Khalistan. In 1799, Maharaja Ranjit Singh established Lahore as the capital of an independent Sikh state where true equality among Sikhs, Muslims, Hindus and others was practised. After his death in 1839, there were problems with the next two leaders and two wars were fought. The British took over the Punjab in 1849 and ended Sikh independence.

When India became independent from Britain in 1947, two countries were established: India was mainly Hindu and Pakistan was mainly Muslim. The Sikh homeland of the Punjab was split between India and Pakistan. Sikhs asked for independence, but it was not given to them.

In 1966, the Indian government agreed that the province of the Punjab should have Punjabi as its official language and that Sikhs should represent the province in the Punjabi Suba (assembly). However, Sikhs are still working to reunite the Punjab into one country of their own.

Learning about religion

1. a   What is meant by equality?

   b   Describe Sikh teaching about equality.

2. a   Explain the Hindu caste system.

   b   Explain why Sikhs believe that the caste system is wrong and how the langar shows this belief in action.

3. Why do Sikhs want a homeland?

Learning from religion

1. Why do you think that some people are not treated equally?

2. Do you think that the Sikh teaching about equality should be adopted by everyone?

3. Explain what you might do to try to make sure that everyone is treated equally.

Service to others 1 – sewa

In this section you will:

- learn about sewa
- learn why this idea is so important to Sikhs
- consider how this teaching might affect people.

It is very important for all **Sikhs** to provide a service to the community – **sewa**. This includes service to the Sikh community itself and to others. Sikhs should be prepared to give up some of their time and energy to help others. Sikhism comprises service to God, to the **Khalsa** and to all of humanity.

Tan – physical service: helping in the langar

Sikhism teaches that a person should try to become less self-centred (**manmukh**) and more God-centred (**gurmukh**), and so live their lives in the selfless service of others (sewa).

Although **Nam Simran**, remembering God, is central to Sikhism, this must be combined with sewa. The following from the **Guru Granth Sahib Ji** emphasizes this point:

> True worship consists in the meditation of God's name… There can be no worship without performing good deeds.
>
> Guru Granth Sahib Ji

There are three different aspects of sewa.

- **Tan** – this is physical service, and might include working in the **langar** and helping to look after the **gurdwara**. Providing langar for the congregation is seen as a privilege as well as a duty.

- Man – this is mental service. Sikhs might do this by studying the Guru Granth Sahib Ji and teaching it to others.

- **Dhan** – this is material service to other people. Sikhs might give money to charities or give their time to help people who are in need. It might also include building a school or a hospital, visiting the sick or caring for disaster victims.

None of these services should be performed for personal gain, but because a Sikh wants to serve God. Therefore, in all of these ways, Sikhs can perform sewa and so serve God and the world.

The **Gurus** themselves set the example of sewa by often performing basic tasks that some people would have considered to be beneath them, for example, cleaning the gurdwara.

Tan – physical service: sweeping the pavements of the Golden Temple

A place in God's court can only be attained if we do service to others in this world… Wandering ascetics, warriors, celibates, holy men, none of them can obtain **mukti** without performing sewa.

Guru Granth Sahib Ji

Learning about religion

1 **a** What is meant by sewa?

b Explain why this is such an important part of Sikhism.

2 **a** Describe how a Sikh might perform different types of sewa to help the community.

b Explain how the Gurus taught sewa by their own example.

3 Explain which you think is the most important of the three types of sewa and also which might be the most difficult to perform.

Learning from religion

1 **a** Do you think that working to help other people is important? Give your reasons.

b Do you think that Sikh teaching about sewa might improve the world if everyone lived by it? Explain your views.

2 Consider whether practising sewa might help you feel closer to God.

3 What sort of sewa do you think you should try to practise in your own life?

Service to others 2

The **Gurus** said that **Sikhs** should live their lives according to three principles, which are all equally important.

● **Nam Simran** – to remember the name of God. This can be done by meditating on God's name.

● **Kirat karna** – to earn a living by honest means.

● **Vand chhakna** – to share everything in charity with people who are less fortunate. This includes time, abilities and money.

These teachings were designed so that Sikhs would not think of the religious side of their lives as being separate from the rest of their lives. Prayer, hard work and generosity are all equally important in living a good life. Sikhs are discouraged from spending all their time on the religious aspects of life – for example, prayer. They must live lives that are complete and that contribute to the welfare of the community.

Kirat karna

Kirat karna means that Sikhs must earn their living honestly. Work is essential for the individual, the family and the community, and a Sikh has a duty to provide for basic needs. Everyone has a responsibility to earn a living if he or she possibly can. It does not matter what the work is, whether it is professional or labouring, provided that it is honest and not against the teachings of the Gurus. Therefore, a Sikh should never earn money from selling illegal drugs or doing something that might take advantage of other people.

Sikhism teaches that it is not wrong to be rich provided the money is gained honestly, but that it is wrong to live your life just in order to make a lot of money. The money a Sikh earns is used for his or her family, and also for the **Khalsa** and the community as a whole.

A Sikh hospital in Nairobi

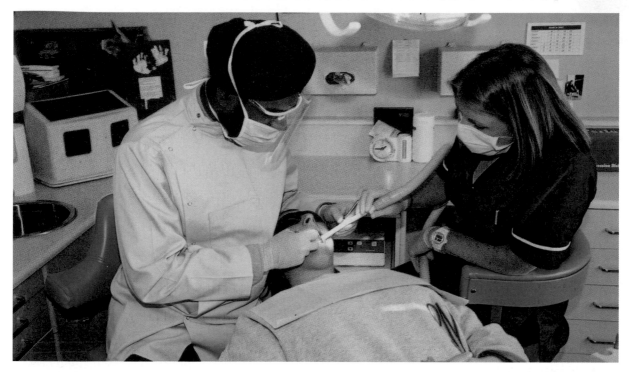

A Sikh dentist can help others through his work

Vand chhakna

Vand chhakna teaches Sikhs that they should live their lives on the principles of generosity and self-sacrifice.

Guru Amar Das Ji taught Sikhs the idea of **daswandh**. This means giving a tenth of surplus money to the community. Money given in this way may be used for building schools or hospitals, or to help those who are poor or suffering. It is up to individuals to decide how much they should give.

Learning about religion

❶ a What is meant by Nam Simran?

b Explain why this is an important part of Sikhism.

❷ a What are Kirat karna and Vand chhakna?

b Explain why these are as important as Nam Simran.

❸ Why are these three concepts important for Sikhs?

Learning from religion

❶ a Do you think that it might be as important to help other people as to pray?

b Do you think that everyone would benefit from the idea of daswandh? Give your reasons.

❷ How might you live in order to follow Kirat karna?

❸ Explain how you would try to ensure that you lived a good life.

Women in Sikhism

In this section you will:

- learn about the Sikh attitude towards women
- think about why this is an important part of Sikh life and teaching
- consider how these attitudes and teachings might affect people.

Sikhism is one of the few religions where women have an equal role with men within the faith.

Within the **Sikh** community, a woman can choose her own way of life, and many Sikh women are now continuing their education to university in order to fulfil their ambition for a professional career.

When there is any suggestion that Sikhism is treating women differently from men, this is because of society and history and it goes against the teachings of the **Gurus**.

Women can be members of the **Khalsa**, undergoing exactly the same ceremony as men, and can become **granthi** – leading the worship in the **gurdwara**.

We are God's own people, neither high nor low nor in between… Religion consists not in mere talk. He who looks on all alike and consider all to be equal is acclaimed as truly religious.

Guru Granth Sahib Ji

Guru Nanak Dev Ji taught that:

From women born, shaped in the womb, to woman betrothed and wed;
We are bound to women by ties of affection, on women man's future depends.
If one woman dies he seeks another; with a woman he orders his life.
Why then should one speak evil of women, they who give birth to kings?
Women also are born from women; none takes birth except from a woman.
Only the True One, Nanak, needs no help from a woman.
Blessed are they, both men and women, who endlessly praise their Lord.
Blessed are they in the True One's court; there shall their faces shine.

Guru Granth Sahib Ji

A woman granthi leading the worship in the gurdwara

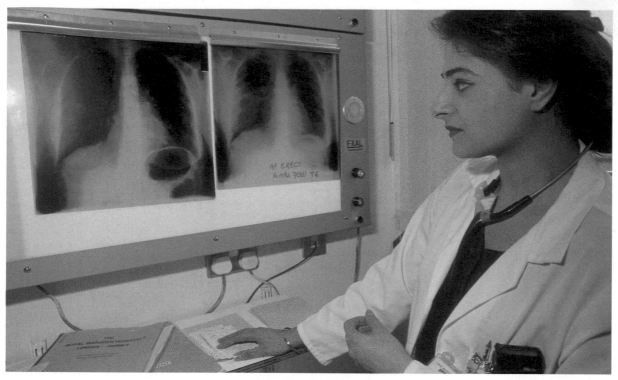

Sikh women are able to work in any field, for example medicine

The Gurus also condemned some Hindu practices, including giving dowries to a man to marry a particular woman, and suttee, the idea that when a man dies his wife should kill herself on his funeral pyre.

Learning about religion

❶ **a** What is meant by sexism?

b How is the Sikh attitude towards women different from that in some other religions?

❷ **a** What did Guru Nanak Dev Ji teach about women?

b Explain the treatment of women that was condemned by the Gurus.

❸ Do you think that Sikh teaching about the role of women is important? Give your reasons.

Learning from religion

❶ **a** Why do you think that some people treat women differently from men?

b Do you think that the Sikh teaching about the role of women should be adopted by other people?

❷ Find out how some other religions regard women.

❸ Consider the view that although women and men are equal, they have different roles to play and so may not be treated the same. Do you agree? Give examples from other religions.

Glossary

Adi Granth a collection of the hymns of the first four Gurus and some of those of Guru Arjan Dev Ji

Akal Takht 'Throne of the Eternal'. The building facing the Golden Temple in Amritsar

Akhand Path a continuous reading of the Guru Granth Sahib Ji from beginning to end

Amrit 'nectar'. Sanctified liquid made of sugar and water, used in initiation ceremonies

Amritsar a city in the Punjab and the location of the Golden Temple

Amritvela early morning prayer and meditation

Anand karaj 'Ceremony of bliss'. The wedding ceremony

Anand Sahib 'Hymn of bliss'

Anandpur Sahib a town in a valley at the foot of the Himalayas. The ashes of the head of Guru Tegh Bahadur Ji are buried there. It is also the place where Guru Gobind Singh Ji founded the Khalsa

Ardas the prayer offered during most religious acts

Asa di var the morning hymn

Baisakhi a major Sikh festival celebrating the formation of the Khalsa, 1699 CE

Bhakti devotion to God, worship

Caste the Hindu belief that people are born into different social groups

Chanani a canopy over the scriptures, used as a mark of respect

Chauri a symbol of the authority of the Guru Granth Sahib Ji. A fan waved over scriptures, made of yak hairs or nylon

Dasam Granth a collection of compositions, some of which are attributed to the tenth Sikh Guru, Guru Gobind Singh Ji, compiled some years after his death

Daswandh giving a tenth of surplus money to the community

Dhan material service to other people

Divali Mela a festival which marks the end of the rainy season and the escape and return to Amritsar of Guru Har Gobind Ji

Diwan congregational worship

Five Ks *see* **Panj kakke**

Goindwal location of a deep well, or baoli, built by Guru Amar Das Ji

Golak a long box in which worshippers place their offering of money

Granthi a reader of the Guru Granth Sahib Ji, who officiates at ceremonies

Gurbani the word of God revealed by the Gurus. Also the Shabads, contained in the Guru Granth Sahib Ji

Gurdwara Sikh place of worship. Literally the 'doorway to the Guru'

Gurmukh someone who lives by the Guru's teaching

Gurmukhi 'from the Guru's mouth'. The name given to the script in which the scriptures and the Punjabi language are written.

Gurpurbs a Guru's anniversary (birth or death). This term is also used for other anniversaries, for example the installation of the Adi Granth, 1604

Guru a teacher. In Sikhism, the title of Guru is used for the ten human Gurus and the Guru Granth Sahib Ji

Guru Granth Sahib Ji the Sikh scriptures, compiled by Guru Arjan Dev Ji and given its final form by Guru Gobind Singh Ji

Guru Nanak Dev Ji (1469–1539) the first Guru and the founder of the Sikh faith

Gutka a collection of Sikh hymns

Harimandir Sahib the Golden Temple in Amritsar

Hola Mohalla Mela festival which celebrates Guru Gobind Singh Ji holding a three-day festival at Anandpur

Hukam 'God's will'

Ik Onkar 'There is only One God'. The first phrase of the Mool Mantar. It is also used as a symbol to decorate Sikh objects